Classic Cornish Anecdotes

Compiled b

GW00492960

Tor Mark Press • Penryn

Introduction

Anecdotes are rare plums in the stodgy pudding of history. Although the stories in this collection have been culled from many sources, some of them serious histories, we do not claim that they are true. They may or may not have happened, but in essence they are the kind of story told in a pub or over dinner, perhaps starting from a real event but often embroidered by the teller, spiced with wit or malice. The range of stories is to some extent governed by the kind of people who recorded them. Inevitably most authors in previous generations were clergy or gentry and there are consequently many anecdotes of eccentric squires or parsons, and regrettably few of miners, fishermen or country people.

It will also be obvious that none of these anecdotes concern living people: we could not afford the libel bills, but fortunately the dead cannot be libelled.

You may find the circumstantial detail will illuminate the Cornish past for you; if so that will be a bonus, but our main hope is that you may find these anecdotes amusing.

First published 1994 by Tor Mark Press,
Islington Wharf, Penryn, Cornwall TR10 8AT

© 1994 Tor Mark Press

ISBN 0-85025-343-8

Acknowledgements

The cover illustration is by Beryl Sanders.

Printed in Great Britain by Burstwick Print and Publicity Services, Hull

Mice in the belfry

Madam Trezillian of Raftra, near Land's End, outdid all other ladies in the county in the extremes of fashion. She had the broadest hoops and above all the highest 'tête' as the tower of cushions, ribbons, lace, wool, pomatum and hair was called, which surmounted ladies *à la mode*. Once these ladies were *en grande toilette*, these monstrous headpieces were not taken down at night, often for weeks on end. Their bedsteads were made a foot or two longer to allow for this.

The parish feastday was a high point of Mrs Trezillian's social calendar, and a barber was sent for from Penzance to construct the highest tête ever seen west of Hyde Park; as the feast lasted all week, naturally Madam did not take down her hair, and then she was reluctant to destroy the wonderful creation. A fortnight or so after the end of the feast she began to suffer from headache, so much so that she sent for Dr Maddron from St Just. He insisted on having the tête taken down and opened. Within it he found a nest of baby mice which had been littered there (no doubt visited nightly by their loving mother) besides any quantity of fly-blows in different stages of growth. Madam's hair was in such a state that she was obliged to have all it shaved off.

Even then, the hair was carefully saved and made into a vast headpiece — for it was more than a wig — which she wore to the next parish feast, which was at Madron. For this event she stayed near Penzance with Squire Daniel and his wife, of Alverton. As she was walking through the market house, the bows of her towering tête caught on the hooks of a butcher's stall, and she walked the full length of the market with great stateliness before discovering from the hoots of the butchers' boys and the laughter all around her that she was revealing a completely bald pate.

More haste, less velocipede

Parson Spry, curate of Sennen and St Levan in the early nineteenth century, was a young man who disregarded convention. Living in Penzance with two widespread parishes to look after and too little money to keep a horse, he bought the newly invented 'velocipede', a primitive bicycle without brakes or pedals. His first trial of the machine was on the outskirts of Penzance, and so proud was he of its speed that next market Thursday he stationed himself at the top of the final hill on the road from St Just and challenged all comers to a race down the hill. Several farmers took up the challenge, but their horses were so frightened that they threw their riders or else bolted over the hedges, anything to avoid the strange beast.

So the parson won his bets, and boasted that his 'horse' was the best in the west. In the last race, however, he was a little over-confident; the horse got quite out of control and he dared not put his legs to the ground to stop it. At the foot of the hill was a stream, and several market women were allowing their horses to drink, while they rested their heavy baskets of butter and eggs on their laps. Among these contented gossips suddenly rushed the parson, tumbling over in the water with the velocipede flying from between his legs. Several of the women were thrown off their horses, which galloped off, some to their accustomed stables, others into the open country. In the stream were broken eggs, shattered jars and floating baskets. In the heat of the moment, the exasperated women pelted him with the ruined butter and remaining eggs and rolled him in the mud, until some gentlemen came to his rescue.

On the following Sunday there was a large audience along the road to St Levan church, hoping to see the parson in action, but they were disappointed for he was indisposed. The next Sunday, however, his wounds and his courage had healed sufficiently for him to set off early. The audience was out again, and they waited a long time; as they were despairing of his arrival, his dog was seen coming towards them. Overjoyed to see people he knew, the dog ran back barking, clearly encouraging them to follow. And there round the corner was the parson, climbing out of a deep pool of mud, with the velocipede still deep within it. He never trusted it again.

Clerical error

The Vicar of Helland sent a message by way of a friend asking the Archdeacon of Cornwall to take a service on his behalf, so that he did not have to return specially for it. The telegram in reply read: 'The Archdeacon of Cornwall is going to Hell and you need not return.'

The death of Spencer Perceval

On the evening of 11 May 1812, Spencer Perceval, Prime Minister and Chancellor of the Exchequer, was shot just as he entered the lobby of the House of Commons, by a man called Bellingham who had concealed himself behind a door.

John Williams, of Scorrier, born in 1753, was the most extensive mining adventurer in Cornwall. On the night Spencer Perceval was killed, Mr Williams had three remarkable dreams, in each of which he saw the whole transaction as distinctly as if he had been there in person. His attested statement relative to these dreams, was drawn up and signed by him in the presence of the Rev. Thomas Fisher and Mr Charles Prideaux Brune.

Mr Williams dreamed that he was in the lobby of the House of Commons and saw a small man enter, dressed in a blue coat and white waistcoat. Immediately after, he saw a man dressed in a brown coat with yellow basket buttons draw a pistol from under his coat and discharge it at the former, who instantly fell, the blood spurting out from a wound a little below the left breast and staining the waistcoat. He heard the report of the shot, and saw the colour of the face change. He saw the murderer seized by some gentlemen who were present, and observed his countenance, and on asking who the gentleman was who had been shot, he was told it was the Chancellor. He then awoke and told his wife Catherine, who very naturally told him it was only a dream and recommended him to be composed and go to sleep again as soon as he could. He did so and shortly woke her again, and said that he had for a second time had much the same dream; whereupon she observed that he had been so agitated by the first dream that she supposed it had dwelt on his mind, and begged him to compose himself and go back to sleep, which he did. A third time the vision was repeated, on which, despite her entreaties that he would be quiet and try to forget it, he arose, it being then between one and two o'clock, and dressed himself.

At breakfast the dreams were the sole subject of conversation; in the afternoon Mr Williams went to Falmouth where he related the particulars of them to all of his acquaintance whom he met. On the following day, Mr Tucker of Trematon Castle, accompanied by his wife, a daughter of Mr Williams, went to Scorrier House about dusk.

Immediately after the first greetings, Mr Williams began to relate his dream to his son-in-law and Mrs Williams observed to her daughter, laughingly, that her husband could not even allow Mr Tucker to be seated before he told him of his nocturnal visitations. Mr Tucker commented that no Lord Chancellor could visit the lobby of the Commons, and asked for a description of the man. Mr Williams described him minutely, to which Mr Tucker replied, 'Your description is not that of the Lord Chancellor, but it is certainly that of Mr Perceval, the Chancellor of the Exchequer; and although he has been to me the greatest enemy I ever met in my life, for a supposed cause which had no foundation in truth, yet I should be exceedingly sorry to hear of his being assassinated.'

Mr Tucker then asked whether Mr Williams had ever seen the

Chancellor and was told that he had never seen him, nor had ever written to him, and in short had had nothing to do with him; nor had he ever been in the lobby of the House of Commons.

During this conversation they heard a horse gallop to the door of the house, and Mr Williams' son Michael Williams entered the room, saying that he had galloped the seven miles from Truro, having seen a gentleman there who had travelled from London on the mail coach. This gentleman had been in the lobby of the Commons on the evening of the 11th, when a man called Bellingham had shot Mr Perceval, and that, as it might occasion a reshuffle of the cabinet which could affect Mr Tucker's political friends, he had come as fast as he could to acquaint him with the news. After the astonishment which this created had a little subsided, Mr Williams described most particularly the appearance of the assassin, as he had already described the victim.

About six weeks later, Mr Williams having business in town went to the House of Commons, where he had never previously been. Immediately he came to the steps at the entrance to the lobby, he said, 'This place is as distinctly familiar from my dream as is any part of my own house.' He pointed to the exact spots at which Bellingham had stood when he fired, and which Mr Perceval had reached when he was struck by the ball, and when and how he fell. The dress, both of Mr Perceval and Bellingham, agreed with the description given by Mr Williams down to the minutest particulars.

These dreams, three times repeated, were not 'tokens', which occur at the precise moment of death; they occurred after the event, but long before Mr Williams had any conventional means of knowing of it.

A rude awakening

The manor of Godolphin was subject to a curious custom. Once a year the reeve of Lambourne came to Godolphin before sunrise on Candlemas Day (2 February), entered the Hall, jumped on a table and stamped his feet to attract attention, then proclaimed 'Oyez, oyez, oyez. I am the reeve of the manor of Lambourne, come to demand the old rent, duties and customs due to the lords of the said manor, from the lands of Godolphin.' Then he received two shillings and eightpence rent, a quart of beer, a loaf of bread and a piece of cheese, which he tasted and then carried away to the lords of the manor of Lambourne.

The origin of this custom is said to have been a snail race, where a St Aubyn and a Godolphin each wagered their properties on the result. The St Aubyn snail took an early lead, and Godolphin attempted to encourage his snail with a pin, but his tipsy aim was awry and the snail 'stopped short never to go again'. So St Aubyn won the Godolphin estate but allowed his friend to retain it subject to the rumbustious custom being maintained.

Apiaric victory

One of the Trevelyans who lived at Bazil, in St Clether, was much in debt and the sheriff with his officers came to arrest him. As he approached the house, Mr Trevelyan saw him coming, bolted the door and retired to an upstairs room, from the window of which he spoke to the sheriff: 'Sir, I guess your business; but I warn you to depart hence within a quarter of an hour, otherwise I will send out my spearmen among your followers.' He then shut the window and retired.

The sheriff and his staff were not to be driven away by idle threats, and waited alertly for the fifteen minutes. Whereupon Mr Trevelyan's head again appeared: 'I perceive, Mr Sheriff, you are not gone; however I will soon make you go.' Thus saying, he threw six or seven hives of bees out of the window, which soon drove the sheriff from the door.

Having the last word

William Milliton and his wife, of Pengersick Castle, did not get on. One day he said, 'Honor, we have lived in wretchedness too long. Let us resolve on a reconciliation, forget the past and agree a new life. And as a pledge of our reunion let us have a feast together tonight.' 'Most certainly, I agree to that,' she replied. So they had a romantic dinner (candle-lit no doubt) prepared just for the two of them and when they had eaten well William proposed a toast to their reconciliation. 'I will drink if you will drink,' she replied, so he drained his flagon and she drained hers. Then she laughed, and said 'William, you have but three minutes to live. Your cup was poisoned!' 'And you,' he responded, 'have five, for yours was poisoned also!'

'That is well,' replied Honor. 'I am content, for I shall have two minutes in which to triumph over your dead carcass, and to spurn it with my foot!'

Wife sales

For poor people in the nineteenth century there was no possibility of divorce, and it was commonly believed among country people in the south-west that a marriage could be ended by the husband 'selling' his wife–often no doubt with her full consent. In 1835, for example, an elderly man named George Trethewey appeared at St Austell market leading his much younger wife by a rope around her waist. Among those interested were two 'tinkers' who travelled together; one of them bid twopence, which was not found acceptable; then the other agreed to add a further twopence, saying they were acting in partnership. This was accepted. The old husband took his fourpence, the collector of market tolls collected a penny fee, and the woman and her two new husbands 'proceeded to a neighbouring pot-house, where they regaled themselves with a jug of ale.'

Later in the century, prices seem to have risen; 2s.6d. bought a wife in 1846, and in 1853 a couple were much disappointed when refused remarriage, since the would-be husband had paid a full sovereign for his bride.

Particularly unfortunate was John Cook of Five Lanes, summoned in 1828 to show why he was not supporting his wife and children. He explained that he had sold his wife for half a crown sixteen years earlier, when she had no children. Since then she had lived with the purchaser and had seven children by him; having become ill, she had applied to the parish. John Cook was found liable to support this family, and if unable to pay up would have been condemned to the treadmill. At the last minute he was acquitted on a technicality.

Hawker stories

The Rev. R.S. Hawker, the famous vicar of Morwenstow, was a man who attracted anecdotes. His eccentricities were many, and he was sufficiently well known to make a new Hawker story immediately interesting to dinner party audiences in Victorian Cornwall and beyond.

Some stories, first told of anonymous parsons, subsequently attached themselves to Hawker: it is said for example that when asked whether he would bury a dissenter he replied, 'Certainly: I should be delighted to bury you all.' Another piece of repartee attributed to him, that when asked whether any doctor ever visited his remote parish he replied, 'No, here we generally die a natural death,' is also attributed to other well-known Cornish characters, such as Ann Glanville, the famous oarswoman of Saltash.

Hawker's poncho

Although undeniably an eccentric, Hawker enjoyed living up to his reputation. One visitor found him wearing 'a peculiar yellow vestment in which he appeared much like a Lama of Tibet, which he wore in his house and about his parish, and which he insisted was an exact copy of a priestly robe worn by St Padarn and St Teilo.' In fact the garment was a yellow rug he had bought in Bideford, with a hole cut through the middle. He had been introduced to this useful garment by a local friend, and it went well with the rest of his accustomed dress: knitted blue sailor's jersey, sea boots above the knee, claret coloured coat and claret coloured hat. He would not wear black: 'Why should we parsons be like crows — birds of ill luck?' he would say.

Strange meats

In 1825 Hawker stayed at the Ship Inn in Boscastle. Asking what was available for dinner (for there were no red menu cards listing the freezer contents in those days) they were told by the landlady, Joan Treworgy, 'Meat.' Asked what kind of meat, she ignored their enquiries, but just replied, 'Meat — nice wholesome meat and taties.'

With little choice, Hawker and his friend sat down to a passable meal, but they couldn't fathom what the roast meat was, for the taste was something like veal, but not veal, and there were no bones to identify it. 'A piece of Boscastle baby?' the vicar speculated, whereupon his friend rushed in horror to the kitchen. He came back shouting 'Meat and taties, meat and taties!'

It was not till years later that Hawker solved the mystery, when he read in an old book that 'the residents of Boscastle and Bossiney do catch in the summer seas divers young seals which, doubtful if they be fish or flesh, cunning housewives will nevertheless roast, and do make thereof savoury meat.'

Pulpitations

When Hawker renovated his church at Morwenstow, he took the panelling out of the pulpit on the grounds that 'the people ought to see the priest's feet'. They also saw his cat, which frequently accompanied him there. He refused to improve the pulpit access, which was through a narrow door and up narrow winding steps, because it typified the camel going through the eye of the needle. The only way to leave the pulpit was to go down the stairs backwards. He was known to whisper to visiting preachers if they got stuck, 'It is a strait and narrow way, and few there are that find it.'

Hawker's views

Plagued, as he thought, by visitors for whom he was as much part of the north coast tour as Boscastle or Bedruthan Steps, and yet whose visits he simultaneously craved, Hawker was once asked for his views. 'There is Hennacliff,' he replied, 'the highest cliff on the coast, on the right; the church on my left, the Atlantic Ocean in the middle. These are my views. My opinions I keep to myself.'

Dissenter at bay

The vicar of Baldhu visited Hawker in 1847 and was told that he had a great aversion to Low Church clergymen and 'dissenters' which was shared by his pet stag, Robin. This animal ranged the rectory lawn and on one occasion had pinned such a creature to the ground with his horns. The poor man cried out in great fear, so Hawker told Robin to let him go which reluctantly he did, 'though he would not hurt him; Robin was kind-hearted.'

Enough wind for one mill

There was only one windmill on the exposed Lizard peninsula. At one time, the story goes, a second was planned. The first miller was concerned and went to see the man who was planning the new mill.

'I say, mate, be you goin' to set up another windmill?'

'I reckon I be; you don't object? There's room for more nor one.'

'Oh, room, room enough! But there mayn't be wind enough to sarve us both.'

Poisoned by William Morris

The Rev. Sabine Baring-Gould was a high Tory squire and parson who wrote books on most subjects under the sun in a wonderfully racy style, and with a tone of total conviction justified rather by his position in society than by his regard for the facts.

In his *Book of Cornwall* he describes the dangers of arsenic manufacture: this was a byproduct of tin ore which became one of the mainstays of the mining industry after the price of tin had fallen catastrophically. Of employees of the Calstock arsenic works who had died, 83% had died of respiratory illness. Baring-Gould had some sympathy for the problem, because at one time he had found his own children troubled with sores about the joints.

'They would not heal. I sent for the local doctor, and he tinkered at them, but instead of mending, the wounds got worse. This went on for many weeks. Suddenly an idea struck me. I had papered some of my rooms with highly aesthetic wall-coverings by a certain well-known artist-poet who had a business in wall-papers. I passed my hand over the wall, and found that the colouring matter came off on my hand. At once I drove into the nearest town and submitted the paper to an analyst. He told me that it was charged with sulphuret of arsenic, and that as the glue employed for holding the paint had lost all its power, this arsenical dust floated freely in the air. I at once sent my children away, and they had not been from home a week before they began to recover. Of course, all the wall-papers were removed.'

The Calstock workers were not so lucky: as the author says, 'Suggestions of remedies have been made, but none practical.'

Salting it away in Saltash

Nicholas Tyack was mayor of Saltash in the time of Oliver Cromwell, and an outspoken supporter of the Commonwealth. But whether through disagreement with the policies of Cromwell, or out of pure self-interest, he found no difficulty at the Restoration of King Charles in disavowing the Commonwealth in terms strong enough to enable him to keep his place.

He used his time as mayor well. Wishing to apprentice his son in London, he took the boy there, lived well during his stay, and charged the expenses to the town. He found it advantageous to live next to the Town Hall, and made a door in the party wall. When the Town Council was to be convened, custom said that the Town Hall bell had to be rung — but the hour at which it was to be rung was not specified nor did custom say that the door had to be unlocked. So when he wished to pass his accounts or carry through some private plan, he rang the bell at night, having forewarned his supporters, and they all trooped from his house into the council chamber to carry his resolutions unopposed.

Fyn and Black Joan

On Looe Island in the eighteenth century lived a man named Fyn and his sister, 'Black Joan'. Children of an outlaw who had been forced to live on the Mewstone rock, they could not bear the idea of mainland life. They dug many tunnels in the rock, and lived by concealing smuggled goods. The customs officers were easily bribed, and a farmer on the mainland used to signal to Fyn by riding a white horse when the coast was clear, or going on foot if the officers were about.

Realising that something of the sort was happening, the Government stationed a guard on the island, which made it difficult to run ashore the large stocks already there. Black Joan ran to this man one day in a great panic: her boat had slipped its moorings and was floating away with the tide. Being a kindly soul (and Joan was after all a young woman) the officer went rowing after her boat and secured it. Meanwhile, on the landward side of the island, a swarm of boats manned by every smuggler in Looe carried the goods to the mainland.

The station on Looe Island never did solve the problem; the Fyns could keep drink flowing liberally (and Joan was after all a young woman) so the officers never quite trusted their man on the island, and 'free trade' continued almost as smoothly as before.

Court positions

Lord Robartes of Lanhydrock made a second marriage to a much younger woman, Letitia Smith who was a great beauty; he was kept at Court by his duties as a minister of the crown. According to Anthony Hamilton, who wrote a scurrilous account of sex life under Charles II, 'Her husband was an old, snarling, troublesome, peevish fellow, in love with her to distraction and to complete her misery always hanging around her.' Perhaps this attentiveness explains why, according to Pepys and others, Lord Robartes fulfilled his administrative duties very sluggishly.

The Duke of York was determined to seduce Letitia. Lord Robartes was offered a number of highly lucrative posts away from Court, such as managing the Duke's Irish revenues or being Lord Lieutenant of Cornwall, always provided he left his wife alone in London for a few months. He refused all these temptations but could see that his young wife was becoming fascinated by the Duke, and for safety took her away into deepest Wales. Thus was virtue preserved and a better story frustrated!

All in the way of Nature

A harvest custom in Cornwall and Devon was to make a loop of straw, and if a boy could catch a girl (or vice versa) and hold her with the loop, then he or she could claim a kiss as a forfeit. This was called making sweet hay. One of the Quaker rules forbade the playing of 'vain sports', and a new young convert, who had been looking forward to harvest, asked timidly whether making sweet hay counted as a vain sport. 'Naw, sure,' was the answer, 'that's a' i' the way o' Natur'.'

Dolly Pentreath stories

Dolly is nowadays famous for not having been the last speaker of the Cornish language, but in her day she was a legendary 'character'. She was known in Mousehole as Dolly the Spring, and was married to a man named Jeffery, but kept her maiden surname as the Pentreaths were a 'better' family than the Jefferys. She was a 'jowster', that is, a pedlar selling fish.

A Cornish curse

Dolly had a reputation for being a bit of a witch, because when excited she seemed to forget her English and revert to her mother tongue, which impressed or frightened people. Meeting a Mr Price riding his horse in a narrow lane one day, she would not give way and he pushed past her, upsetting her baskets. She cursed him in Cornish ('*Cronnack an hagar dhu!*') and he was so scared that he bought all her fish to placate her; but he was still worried about the curse, so much so that he paid her half a crown to translate what she had said. When she had the coin in her hand, she said 'You ugly black toad!' He was so furious he made to horsewhip her but she told him she would put a spell on him, so he had to back down.

Dolly Pentreath and the wickedest tongue

Walking back to Mousehole from Penzance, Dolly noticed four schoolboys behind her, chanting by turns the Greek alphabet which they were trying to learn — 'alpha,' 'beta,' 'kappa,' 'delta'. Suddenly she took to her heels, and they were astonished to see her rush into the school. When they arrived, she was complaining vociferously to the schoolmaster that violence had been offered her by four of his boys. She had heard them saying, 'At her!' 'Beat her!' 'Damn her!' 'Pelt her!'

When the master had explained her mistake, she said 'If that's a sample of the outlandish tongue, then it's the wickedest I've ever heard.'

Dolly in her tub

A deserter from a man o'war fled to Dolly Pentreath's house for refuge, and she was willing enough to hide him. In the chimney there was a cavity large enough for a man so she pushed him into it, drew a bundle of dry furze onto the fire and filled the big pot with water. Into the middle of the kitchen she pulled the 'keeve' she used as a washtub. When the Lieutenant and his men entered the cottage in hot pursuit of the deserter, Dolly was in her shift, bare-legged and

13

ready to wash her feet. She screamed at them that she was washing and was just waiting for the water to boil, but the officer persisted. She 'gave tongue in strong and forcible Cornish' and then went to the door and roused the neighbours: this Lieutenant was quite impudent enough to ransack every cottage! The outcry and the assembling crowd persuaded the officer to withdraw, and that night a lugger stole out of Mousehole carrying the fugitive to Guernsey.

A wrinkled, yet delicious, morceau

Dr John Wolcot, after a career as a doctor in south Cornwall, made a name for himself in London as a writer of satirical mock-heroic poetry, under the pen-name Peter Pindar. One of his poems celebrates Dolly, and her 'discovery' by the antiquarian Daines Barrington. Here is part of the poem, with the author's footnote, which suggests a new light on this momentous meeting and sturdy contempt for early signs of the heritage industry:

'Hail Mousehole! birthplace of old Doll Pentreath,*
The last who jabber'd Cornish, so says Daines.
Daines! who a thousand miles unwearied trots
For bones, brass farthings, ashes and old pots,
To prove that folks of old, like us, were made
With heads, eyes, hands and toes, to drive a trade.

*A very old woman of Mousehole, supposed (falsely however) to have been the last who spoke the Cornish language. The honourable antiquarian Daines Barrington Esq journeyed, some years since, from London to the Land's End to converse with this wrinkled, yet delicious, *morceau.* He entered Mousehole in a kind of triumph and, peeping into her hut, exclaimed with all the fire of an enraptured lover, in the language of the famous Greek philosopher — 'Eureka!' The couple kissed — Doll soon after gabbled — Daines listened with admiration — committed her speeches to paper, not venturing to trust his memory with so much treasure. The transaction was announced to the Society — the journals were enriched with their dialogues — the old lady's picture was ordered to be taken by the most eminent artist, and the honourable member to be publicly thanked for their discovery.'

A marriage on the rocks

A certain Mr Trefusis, of Trefusis, prided himself on his marksmanship; he offered a boy a guinea for allowing him to shoot at a mark directly above the boy's head, in the style of William Tell but with a pistol. The boy survived, but the ordeal brought on a series of epileptic fits.

The same gentleman one day invited his wife for a boating trip. Towards the mouth of Carrick Roads, between Pendennis Point and St Mawes, lies the Black Rock, exposed at most stages of the tide but covered at high tide when a large buoy marks the spot. Mr Trefusis wished to picnic on the rock. When he had landed his wife, he made a bow and rowed away saying, 'Madam, we are mutually tired of each other, and you will agree with me that it were best to part.'

Fortunately a fishing smack picked her up just as the tide was lapping round her ankles, and took her back to Trefusis. 'Be hanged to you rogues,' said the husband. 'I'd have given you a guinea each to have let her drown; now you shan't have a shilling from me.'

The procedure

An inexperienced young curate was with some locals when a drowned seaman was washed ashore.

'What is the procedure?' he asked.

'Sarch is pockets,' was the prompt reply.

Tillie decayed

Sir James Tillie, of Pentillie Castle on the banks of the Tamar, built himself a tower called Mount Ararat. In his will he instructed that when he died (which was in 1714) he was not to be buried, but strapped into his chair and dressed in his best clothes, wig and hat. He was convinced, who knows through what dabblings in alchemy or religion, that he would within two years return to his body. He didn't. The all too mortal remains were in time put into a coffin, and buried within the tower.

Buttock in a china ship

A ship was wrecked on the Hayle side of Carrick Gladden in the late eighteenth century. It had been on a smuggling run and when it beached the crew made off as fast as they could, taking the ship's papers but without time to remove the cargo, which included porcelain, at that time carrying a heavy tax.

A customs officer, Roger Wearne, went aboard from a small boat and, seeing his opportunity, stuffed a fair quantity of porcelain into his baggy trousers. Then he backed down the side of the ship into the boat, but with such caution that one of his companions grew impatient and playfully thwacked him across the backside with an

oar, shouting, 'Look sharp, Wearne!' The boat crew were as astonished by the sound of breaking china as by the howl from Wearne
when the fragments sliced into his flesh.

Queen Elizabeth and the pox

It is often said that German mining experts were brought to Cornwall
in Tudor times to instruct the Cornish in the latest techniques. Then
as now, Cornishmen did not think highly of advice from foreign-
ers and concluded that their own techniques were superior. One
name which crops up again and again as a German advisor is that
of Burchard Cranach. Richard Carew, son of the historian, listened
agog to the following story, told at his father's dinner table.

Burchard Cranach's reputation as a mining advisor was sinking
fast, because his excavations always collapsed just as the ore lodes
were reached. He had a useful sideline as a doctor. In this he was
more successful, and a series of recommendations led to him going
to London in 1562, 'minded' by a Carew retainer because he wasn't
trusted. There he cured Lord Hunsdon and ultimately was called
in to see Queen Elizabeth, who was clearly in the early stages of
some illness. After the consultation, he told her, 'My liege, thou shalt
have the pox.' She was so offended that she called immediately,
'Have away the knave out of my sight!'

She then fell so sick that none of her doctors dared visit her (it
was considered unlucky to be the last doctor to see a dying
monarch!) and as a last resort Burchard was again sent for. Carew's
servant, Roach, announced the arrival of two courtiers with a spare
horse. Cranach fell into a rage, swearing, 'By God's pestilence, if she
be sick, then let her die. Call *me* knave for my good will!' Roach was
persuasive. He took out his dagger: 'Dispatch, for one way or the
other you shall quickly go!' Cranach, still in a fury, pulled on his cassock and boots, snatched from the cupboard a bottle of liquor, flung
himself downstairs and onto the spare horse, and reached the palace
gates well ahead of the courtiers.

His first words to the Queen were, 'Almost too late my liege!'
He had a pallet bed made up before the blazing fire, had her
enveloped (all but one hand) in the scarlet cloth which was then a
vital aspect of fever treatment and suggested she took a drink from
his bottle. This bedside manner and the first swig of the liquor both
appealed to the Queen, and she consented to drink the rest of the
bottle. Promptly red spots rose on the exposed hand.

'What is this, Mr Doctor?'

'Tis the pox.' At which, when she complained that she loathed that disease, he replied, 'By God's pestilence, which is better, to have the pox in the hands, in the face and in the arse, or have them in the heart and kill the whole body?' And she recovered, except that the smallpox so disfigured her that ever afterwards she wore thick make-up.

As a reward she gave him a pair of golden spurs, and land in Cornwall confiscated from a Catholic. However, to be be offered a reward by a Tudor monarch was one thing, to receive it another thing entirely. The prudent Lord Burghley, thinking of the state of the nation, prevented the gift. Burchard's rage was extreme but powerless: 'She queen over him! and he deny me what she give me? No, he be king over her, me care not for it.'

Half-drowned and then roasted

Samuel Drew, a self-educated writer, took part in at least one smuggling run, at Crafthole in 1784, in company with just about every man in the village. He was in an open boat when one of his companions lost his hat overboard, lunged for it and upset the boat. It was a black night (the best for a run) and in the dark Drew and two others clung to the upturned hull, not knowing which way to swim; their three companions drowned. At length they were able to distinguish some rocks and to clamber onto them but by this stage they were so cold and exhausted that they could do no more than hang on there while the sea washed over them.

Once they had rested a while, they shouted for help but the other villagers, in greed or fear for their own safety, insisted on fully unloading the cargo before putting off again to rescue the half drowned men from the rocks. Eventually they were removed to a farmhouse, where they were placed in the chimney recess and forced to endure the heat which their rescuers thought necessary to bring them back to life. Drew wrote, 'My first sensation was that of extreme cold. It was a long time before I felt the fire, though its effects are still visible on my legs, which are burnt in several places. The wounds continued open more than two years, and the marks I shall carry to the grave.'

Language problem

In 1718, the Rev. Daniel Lombard was granted a Cornish living on the presentation of the Prince of Wales. As this was just after the Hanoverian succession, the Prince was of course a German; Lombard was a French Huguenot, educated partly at Oxford, who had spent most of his life in Germany. As such, he was even more at a loss to communicate with the Cornish than were Englishmen of the day. He set off from Exeter for his living at 'Lanteglos iuxta Camelford' with a servant, two spare horses and no adequate road map (though that was hardly his fault, since in those days there were not enough roads for anyone to have found them worth mapping). He enquired many times in his heavy German accent for Lan Deglo juxta Karmelvore. Those questioned, convinced he must be a tourist and that tourists then as now have just one aim in view, kept telling him it was just one day further and directed him onwards until he reached Land's End.

He was reputed not to be a man of the world and apocryphal stories abounded, for example that when observing sheep with ruddle marks, he was concerned that they were red hot; and seeing a hen with a vast brood of chicks, he was amazed that she should have milk for so many.

The curse of Psalm CIX

Thomas Thomas of Gwinear died of a broken heart. He had been courting a cousin, Elizabeth Thomas, and they were believed to have 'an understanding'. But following a tiff, and perhaps out of resentment, he escorted another young woman to chapel on Sunday. This was on 31 May 1772. While they were there, Elizabeth hanged herself, leaving a message that he should consult Psalm 109 —'They have rewarded me evil for good, and hatred for my love.... Let his children be fatherless and his wife a widow....' and many other uncharitable imprecations.

Thomas believed himself ruined for ever. He was no longer able to bear the sight of his native village and moved away to Marazion; but he could not escape his thoughts. If Sunday fell on the 22nd of the month, the day when Psalm 109 was appointed to be read, he could not go to divine service nor attend any Bible reading group in case it was referred to. He began to see visions of Elizabeth staring at him malevolently.

When, with his mind deranged as it was, he tried courting other girls, one after another they asked whether he wanted to bring the curses of Psalm 109 on them; but at length he found a woman less superstitious than the rest. As he led her to St Hilary church to be married, a sudden and violent wind struck them, which is not an infrequent occurrence in Mounts Bay. But he was convulsed with terror, quite literally married in fear and trembling, believing that his former lover had ridden the whirlwind. Before long, his body as well as his mind was destroyed with guilt: he died aged 37 and was buried the following Sunday. It was the 22nd, so while his body lay in the church awaiting burial, the congregation listened to Psalm 109.

Gaiters sucked off on Bodmin Moor

Although smaller than Dartmoor, the trackless expanse of Bodmin Moor is in some ways more dangerous, especially with its bogs. The Rev. Baring-Gould was almost lost in one in 1891:

'The Ordnance Survey Office had sent down an official to go over and correct the map of this district and I was with him. When dusk set in we started for Five Lanes and lost our way. We both got into Redmire, and had to trip along warily from one apparently firm spot to another. The winter and summer had been unusually wet, and the marsh was brimming with water. Six bullocks had already been lost in it that year.

'All at once I sunk above my waist, and was being sucked further down. I cried to my companion, but in the darkness he could not see me, and had he seen me he could do nothing for me. The water finally reached my armpits. Happily I had a stout bamboo, some six feet long, and I placed this athwart the surface and held it with my arms as far expanded as possible. By jerks I gradually succeeded in lifting myself and throwing my body forward, till finally I was able to cast myself full length on the surface. The suction had been so great as to tear the leather gaiters I wore off my legs. I lay full length gasping for nearly a quarter of an hour before I had breath and strength to advance, and then wormed myself along on my breast till I reached dry land.'

Lady Edgcumbe rises from the grave

The Edgcumbe family were residing at Cotehele (or Cuttell as our source spells it) and Lady Edgcumbe had just expired. Her body had been deposited with much ceremony in the family vault. That very night the sexton, hoping to salvage a little jewellery from the grave, went down into the vault with a dark lantern and, observing a gold ring on her ladyship's finger, attempted to pull it off. Not succeeding he was pressing and pinching the finger and tugging at the hand — when the body stirred in the coffin. The man ran off in terror, leaving his lantern behind him. Her ladyship arose and, taking the lantern, tottered to the mansion. It was some five years later, in 1680, that her son Sir Richard Edgcumbe, later first Baron Edgcumbe, was born.

Black sheep and widows

'The manor of Cardinham was customary, freehold or copyhold lands for life, and there was a peculiar tenure respecting widows, who forfeited their lands in the case that they deviated from the paths of chastity; but who might again recover them by submitting to the following penance. She had to attend the manor court riding upon a black sheep, and while in this position she confessed her incontinency to the steward in a sort of slang doggerel, and pleading penance, prayed she might have her lands again. This ceremony being performed, the steward was bound by custom to re-admit her to the free-bench.'

Theatre of war

In the year 1565, a company of itinerant players staying at Penryn happened one night to be representing a battle on the stage, just as a party of Spaniards had secretly landed to attack and plunder the town. The enemy, hearing the clamour of the drums and trumpets of the players, and supposing the townsmen were alarmed and preparing for their reception, rapidly retreated to their boats, after firing a few shots by way of bravado. Thus were the inhabitants delivered from impending dangers without incurring any personal risk.

The wisest punner in Christendom

King James I of England enjoyed watching the gentlemen and (to a lesser extent) the ladies of his court dancing. On one occasion a lively gentleman of the Erisey family from the Lizard was dancing in the King's presence when his hat was jerked from his head and fell to the ground. Without disturbing the rhythm of the dance, he retrieved it with his toe and tossed it back onto his head, much to the admiration of all who saw it. The King enquired who the active gentleman was, and being told his name was Erisey, said 'I like the gentleman very well, but not his name of Heresy.'

One handed Carew

John Carew, second son of the historian, inherited the manor of Penwarne in Mevagissey parish. In 1601, at the siege of Ostend, John Carew lost his right hand to a passing cannon ball, an event which he took most stoically. Returning to his lodgings for an early shower, he threw the amputated hand on the table remarking to the hostess, 'This is the hand that cut the pudding today.' One-handed Carew, as he was known, had an artificial hand contrived from elastic and springs, and after his death his portrait and the artificial hand were both preserved at Heligan.

A cranky paddle boat

Mr Charles Warwick, a lawyer in Truro of eccentric habits, constructed a boat of lightweight materials, covered either with canvas or water-proofed paper; on each side was a paddle wheel, connected to a central crank, much as is now found on children's boating lakes. This was in the late eighteenth century, when paddle boats had yet to be invented. In this craft he made excursions from Truro as far as Falmouth, working the crank manually and outpacing all other craft.

Too much foreknowledge

The last Trecarrel of Trecarrel, Lezant, started building a great mansion, the kind of building for which his descendants would bless him. He was a man very learned in the sciences, especially astronomy and its then companion art, astrology. When his son was about to be born and his wife went into labour, he cast the child's horoscope and found it most unfavourable, portending a short life and an accidental death.

He rushed to his wife's room, and begged the midwife one way or another to delay the birth at least one hour. But this was not possible, and the baby was born to general rejoicing — except from his father. The boy grew most promisingly until one day the maid, leaving the toddler alone while she fetched a dry towel for his bath, returned to find him head down in the ewer of water, quite dead.

Trecarrel abandoned his building work, and instead spent most of his fortune on the improvement and repair of the neighbouring churches, most notably Launceston.

'Go to Launceston!'

A gentleman famous for his benevolence and kindness was one night unusually restless and quite unable to sleep. He told his wife, 'I seem to hear, as plainly as if you said it, a voice sounding in my ears: go to Launceston, go to Launceston.' His wife gave him the normal matrimonial reassurances — that it was all nonsense, and would he just forget it and let them both get some sleep.

But the voice continued and in the middle of the night he got up, saddled his horse and rode off. It was a foul night with a strong gale blowing. He had to cross a ferry; the passage was rough and the boatman said 'Sir, it's as well you were not a minute later, or it would have been too dangerous to cross.' So he arrived at Launceston, still unaware of why he was there, and took an early breakfast at the White Hart. It was crowded because the assizes were to be held that day. There he learned that a soldier was to be tried for deserting his post and conniving at a robbery; having no business to attend to, he went along to the trial.

The evidence was overwhelming, although nowadays it might be regarded as too circumstantial to convict. The soldier insisted that he had been awake and at his post on the cliff; he had seen a gentleman walking along the shore below in the moonlight and exchanged words with him, just as the clock struck midnight — the hour of the crime. But he did not know who the man was.

It was, of course, the benevolent gentleman, who was able to speak up in court and obtain the innocent man's acquittal.

Dialect stories

Many traditional Cornish comic stories were told at the expense of named (but usually fictional) people who were apparently fools or immensely naive, but often had a core of good sense. The tone of these stories, and the rendering of the dialect in which they were narrated, can now seem condescending, but here are three from the collection of I.T. Tregellas, so that you can judge for yourself.

Joe Teague was ill and the druggist prescribed mercury ointment to be rubbed in. Having paid his twopence, Joe asked how much to rub in.

'A piece about the size of a pea.'

'Size of a pea,' said Joe; and again repeated it as he descended the steps, and then again louder: 'How 'bout the size of a pee, that's no size at all, you haven't told me nothing. Size of a pee? Why, come here, doctor. Over there is a small P and there's another there, but the P in Pearce the painter's sign is as large as a loaf of bread, and I can't rub in that from this here little box full.'

'You stupid,' replied the druggist. 'I didn't mean the letter P, I meant a pea that grows in the garden.'

'Then don't call me stupid,' said Joe, 'for if you hadn't been stupider than I, you'd have called it by the right name, which isn't a pea but a *pay* or when we eat a good many of them we call them *paysen.*'

Cousin Ellic was in a successful fishing party, and his share of the catch included a large ling, weighing a good twenty-five pounds.

Determined to sell it, he went to the parish barber-surgeon and dropped it right on the surgeon's boots.

'There, doctor, there's a beauty for 'ee; that's the largest ling that's been catched here for years; he do weigh nigh 'pon thirty pound, and you shall have 'un for a shillin'. 'Tes oal I goat for the night.'

But the doctor had no need for the fish and would not buy, despite all that Cousin Ellic did to persuade him, with a persistence that exhausted the surgeon's patience; and this left Ellic thinking that barter was the only way forward in the negotiation.

'What do you sell, doctor, that I can eat?'

'Poison!' roared the doctor.

'That won't do,' said Ellic. 'I'll change with 'ee meat for meat, and have no money.'

'I won't have your fish at any price.'

'Oh, what shall I do?' groaned Ellic. 'What do you charge to pull a tooth?'

'A shilling,' replied the surgeon.

'I suppose toothache is sure to come,' said Ellic, 'and I'll have one drawed afore it do come, and that'll make us quits for the ling.'

'Agreed,' said the surgeon; and after a few painful tugs, Ellic was free of his sound tooth and his troublesome fish.

'Un Bettun' (Aunt Betty) Cock was a midwife who continued working till she was over eighty, and frankly rather past it:

Un Bettun used to go round to groanings and have some caudle, which she said should be pretty strong of gin and sugar; and she oalways used to say the cheeld was like the faather, whe'er 'twas so or no, and keeped on saying the saame tell she was too blind to knaw a cheeld from a craadle. So when I seed her coming, I towld my wife that the owld decaiver was coming and I wud sarve her a trick, and so I ded, for I took the cheeld up out of the craadle and put 'un in bed, and took the billies [bellows] into the craadle, and when Un Bettun comed in, I was rockin' away for life.

'How are 'ee?' says Un Bettun, and oal like that. 'Let's see the cheeld,' say she.

'Then you musn touch 'un' says I 'for I've been rockin' of un tell I'm tired, and I waan't have un waaked.'

'I waan't wake un,' says she. 'I'll only look 'pon his faace.'

Weth that she went over to the craadle and pulled down the cloathes a bit, and seed the kep, when she beginned, 'Aw what a beauty a es!' and oal like that.

'And who do ee think he's like, Un Bettun?' says I.

'Like?' says she, 'why he's a beauty!' says she, 'and zackly like the faather.'

I loffed of coose, and then I gov her some caudle.

Father Wason's hat

Cornwall in the nineteenth and early twentieth centuries had its share of clergy who sought to restore High Church practices, perhaps in an effort to stem the tide of Methodism. Many of them combined their love of ornate ceremonial with distinctly eccentric personal beliefs and behaviour. Hawker was one, but Father Wason of Cury was a comparable intriguing oddity.

His friend Bernard Walke (whose *Twenty Years at St Hilary* is a delightful book) was invited with his wife to a dinner party. They cycled over, arrived tired, and found a notice on the door. 'No one to enter.' In due course Father Wason arrived from the garden with his cassock tucked up and his arms full of irises. He did not invite them in, just muttered in passing, 'Colour scheme all wrong, must get it right for Dod Procter.'

A further wait followed, then from an upstairs window Father Wason shouted, 'Table all wrong without a black centre. Am looking for my tall hat.' After yet a further delay, he threw open the front door and greeted them as though they had just that minute arrived. On the dining table was the tall black hat, used as a vase, and looking, apparently, so perfectly proper for this purpose that the guests wondered why hats were not in general use as table decorations.

Captain Tom and the robin

Captain Tom Osborne of Balawenath succumbed to pleurisy and pneumonia; at first he just rolled about angrily in bed, fretting about the broccoli which needed harvesting, but then he grew weaker and weaker and lost all interest in his family and his farm; he appeared certain to die.

While the vicar sat by the sleeping man one day, he was horrified to see a robin fly in through the open window. In west Cornwall a robin in a sick room was regarded as a certain sign of approaching death, and if Captain Tom saw the bird, he might well have had a heart attack, so the vicar got up to shoo the bird away. As he did so, Captain Tom woke up, hauled himself up on his pillows, which he had been too weak for several days to do, and stared at the bird of ill omen, perched on the end rail of his bed.

Coughing chestily, he shouted to the bird, 'Get out, you bugger, you've come to the wrong house,' and sank back, whispering an apology for his bad language, but with a smile on his lips.

His wife ran into the room: when she heard there had been a robin in the room she said, 'That's a terrible sign, for it means death.' 'Not for Tom,' replied the vicar. 'It'll take more than a robin to kill him.' And indeed it did; perhaps because of the confrontation, Tom recovered first his interest, then his appetite, then his strength, and within a few days was out and about on the farm again.

The terrific Trevithick

Richard Trevithick the great inventor was a man of fabled strength. His feats included writing his name on a beam six feet above ground with a 56 pound weight attached to his thumb, and tossing a sledge hammer right over an engine house.

The dining room of the Count House at Dolcoath mine was preserved long after it was obsolete as a monument to another exploit. One Captain Hodge, a burly six footer, fancied his chances of wrestling with Trevithick. In one quick rush, Trevithick seized him, upturned him and printed the marks of his boots into the ceiling.

Crusty Pye

A vicar of Truro in the eighteenth century, the Rev. Pye, disliked visiting clergy preaching at too great length. He would stand up in his pew, holding his watch, and proclaim that his roast loin of veal was in danger of spoiling.

One Sunday, just as the town Corporation were passing down the steps to the vestry in ceremonial procession, and the organ was bursting into a roar, the vicar's attention was distracted by looking at the Tables of Consanguinity which were publicly displayed. 'A man may not marry his grandmother,' he proclaimed, and then added after a pause, 'Damn fool if he did.'

The magic straw bales

Harry Warne was a Polperro 'conjurer', renowned for finding missing objects. He was a lazy but popular man, a cheerful companion and prepared to turn his hand to any task that needed doing. He dropped in one day on a farmer and agreed, in exchange for a dinner, to spin some thatching straw. By dinner-time Harry had spun two bundles so huge that he was assumed to have used his magic powers. A few days later, the same farmer had to call in Harry as a conjurer, to locate two missing pack saddles, presumed stolen. 'No,' said Harry, 'not stolen; they'll turn up after the harvest.' And indeed they did, because when harvest was done and other tasks such as thatching the outbuildings could be tackled, the two massive bundles soon revealed the saddles.

Now where was I?

A parson at Kenwyn was reading the second lesson when he saw two dogs fighting at the west end. There was nothing unusual in this, because pets were often brought into church; but suddenly he realised that one was his own. He rushed down the aisle, parted the dogs, and returned breathless, asking the clerk, 'Roger, where was I?' 'Why, down parting the dogs, maister,' said Roger.

Tailor cut

Polwhele, the Cornish historian and snob, tells the tale of an exclusive London tailor named Trist who kept almost open house with food and drink for Cornish gentlemen visiting the capital. Sir Francis Bassett seemed almost to live there. But when Trist happened to be travelling past Tehidy, home of the Bassetts, he was sent to the steward's hall for his dinner, with the servants. He never condescended again to make a garment for Sir Francis.

Let's all start fair

'At no great distance from St Anthony, a wreck happening on a Sunday morning, the parish clerk announced to the congregation just assembled that "Maister wud gee them a holladay." This is fact. But whether maister cried out as his flock were rushing out of the church, "Stop, stop, let's all start fair," I will not aver.' From Polwhele's *Traditions and Recollections*, 1826.

Reverend Maggoty Pie

Parson Karkeek of Truro sounds to have been a disagreeable man. He was for ever nagging his congregation, and also taunted and played tricks on Crety Hooper, a mantua-maker who habitually stuttered. Meeting her carrying a jug of milk in the street, he began his usual raillery, mimicking her stuttering. She had had enough: this time she flung the contents of the jug all over him, exclaiming, 'Thee were a rook before, I've now made thee a magotty pie [magpie].'

Pony trap trap

In his perceptive study of R.S. Hawker, Piers Brendon tells a story about his own grandfather, a yeoman farmer who generally returned home to Stratton from Holsworthy market rather the worse for drink.

The pony knew the way back perfectly well, so the farmer could safely fall asleep while driving the trap. Unfortunately, however, the pony was unable to unlatch the gate so they often waited outside till morning. On one occasion, his sons stole down in the night, unhitched the pony, took it through the gate and re-hitched it, so that when grandad woke up he and the trap were on one side of the gate and the pony was on the other. He never referred to the incident: perhaps he blamed the piskies!

We bain't at sea now

'When the old coaches, better known as buses, plied between town and town in the county, I made many a pleasant journey in them. One morning a company of Porthleven fishermen having taken almost entire possession of the inside of one of these conveyances, bound from Helston to Falmouth, their first act was to close every opening which admitted air, excepting of course the entrance. Being inside I made a mild protest and pleaded for the opening of at least one panel. All in vain; with perfect good humour they held their ground, assuring me that an open window must surely give every man among them a cold.

'"But," I argued, "a fisherman must be impervious to cold, being exposed day and night at sea in all weathers."

'"It baint the same, maester, it baint the same; and we aint at sea now," was all I could get from them. So we endured, with as good a will as possible; but I found it hard to get from my mind the absurdity of the idea that the same man may be a Spartan at sea and a valetudinarian ashore. Trying to solve this problem, and overcome by the heat, I dropped asleep.' From *Cornwall - Forty Years After* by J.S. Flynn.

Seed off

A miner near St Blazey was honorary Treasurer of the local chapel. He had built up quite a sum in the kitty towards repairs on the building and three youths broke into his home to rob him. They found him at his kitchen table, with a candle and a pile of powder which they took to be gunpowder — common enough in Cornwall then, when so many men were self-employed miners. He threatened to blow them all up if they attempted to take the money, so they threw themselves on his mercy. They were previously of good character, and he promised not to report the incident to the police if they would undertake to go regularly to chapel; which they did. He later revealed that the 'gunpowder' had been leek seed.

A receipt for the prevention of toothache in gentlefolk

Richard Carew the younger, son of the historian, was something of a hypochondriac. Observing that his young daughters had no toothache, whilst he had it badly, and that their noses were always running, whereas his was dry, he concluded that if only he could 'expel the rheum from the gums, which, having forced a passage there through that flesh, should naturally have vented itself by the nose', then he too would be freed from pain. First he tried sneezing powder, but that was too violent. Then he put twin rolls of tobacco up his nostrils, which made him so dizzy that he staggered around like a drunken man, his ears thundered and he vomited. Despite these side-effects, he knew he was on the right track, and tried the same again, but this time lying with a blanket over his head and a 'warming stone' at his feet (his own invention, acting like a hot-water bottle) and so he sweated it out. The effect was, he reported, to cure his toothache, check dental decay and improve his general health.

A model Puritan husband

This same Richard Carew lacked those characteristics of humour and warmth which make his father's writing so delightful. When his first-born son died, only a few weeks after birth, 'it made me remember my sins, which it pleased God to punish by the death of that infant.' His wife was away from home, and he had to break the news to her; initially he had hoped to do so gradually, but she guessed immediately and broke down. 'When I found her apt to grieve too much, I told her I humbly thanked God that He had given *me* His grace to take this trial patiently, by which I was assured He would give me another son; if she too would be patient, it would be by her, if *not*, by somebody else.'

Massiful Anthony Payne

During the Civil War, neighbours and families were bitterly divided. After the battle of Stamford Hill, Anthony Payne of Stratton, 'the Cornish Giant', was helping collect up the bodies of the dead, and bury them ten to a trench. It was no problem to him to carry in a corpse under one arm, but one such 'corpse' started pleading with him, 'Surely Mr Payne, you wouldn't bury me before I am dead?'

'I tell thee, man, our trench was dug for ten and there's nine in it already; you must take your place.'

'But I bean't dead, I say; I haven't done living yet. Be massiful Mr Payne; don't ye hurry a poor fellow into the earth before his time.'

'I won't hurry thee: I mean to put thee down quietly and cover thee up, and then thee canst die at thy leisure.'

But in fact, he carried the wounded man to his own cottage and there his wife tended to the man's wounds, and the man survived; his descendants continued to live in Stratton, and perpetuated the story.

Our Coronation

Edward VII was due to be crowned, and throughout the land preparations had been made for this overdue event. At the last minute the king fell ill with appendicitis and the great event had to be postponed.

'Corornation postponded?' cried one elderly man on the celebrations committee of a Cornish town. Our Corornation postponded? I never 'eerd tell o' no such thing in all me life! Why, all the buns is ordered! Whatever shall us do ef there edden no Corornation? I tell 'ee shure nuff, we'll have our Corornation just the same.'

And with a fine disregard for this provocation from up-country, go ahead they did.

Dog eat dog

A Penzance solicitor owned a large dog which he allowed to run loose: it was in the habit of roaming through the market and stealing joints of meat from the stalls. One day, one of the butchers went to the solicitor and asked whether he could sue the owner of a dog which had stolen a leg of mutton from his stall. 'Certainly, my good man.' 'Then, please sir, the dog is yours and the price of the mutton is 4s.6d.' The solicitor promptly agreed to pay and the butcher was going away in triumph, when he was called back: 'Stay a moment, my good man, a lawyer's consultation costs 6s.8d. You owe me the difference.' So the discomfited butcher had to pay up instead.

Cromwell's skull

In his *Around Helston in the Old Days* A.S. Oates tells a story of Helston Fair. A travelling showman called Maxwell had a portable box, supported by a strap round his neck, into which for the price of a penny you could look at 'Oliver Cromwell's skull'. A man who had paid his penny remarked, 'It's a funny thing, Mr Maxwell, I've a photo of Oliver Cromwell at home in an old book and he's pictured as having a very large head. The skull you have on show is a very small one. How do you account for that?' Maxwell replied, promptly enough, 'Oh, this was his skull when he was a boy.'

'Abhor it as a deadly poison'

Methodists are generally thought of as tea-totallers. In 1746 their founder John Wesley appealed to all Methodists, 'You have need to abhor it as a deadly poison, and to renounce it from this very hour.' He was speaking not of the demon alcohol, but of tea. His own experience as an undergraduate and his observation that many in his London congregation suffered from shaking hands and bad nerves had led him to believe (and modern medical opinion would agree) that tea contains an addictive drug which can easily have ill effects.

Charles Wesley was in Cornwall when his brother's appeal arrived, and his diary describes classic withdrawal symptoms: 'I began my week's experiment of leaving off tea; but my flesh protested against it. I was but half awake and half alive all day, and my headache so increased towards noon that I could neither speak nor think. So it was for the two following days, with the addition of a violent purging...'

In Cornwall, where tea was comparatively cheap because smuggled, the addiction proved too strong for the Wesleys to crack.

Wesley's flirtations

John Wesley was something of a ladies' man, though this was of course hushed up by his followers. He was in the habit of kissing all the ladies before retiring to bed. He also flirted extensively with Mrs Mary Pendarves, a widow who had been unwillingly married at the age of 17 to Alexander Pendarves of Roscrow, more than forty years older than her and notorious for his bright red face and unrefined manners. (It was his kinsman Sir Walter Pendarves who invited his friends around to drink brandy from a copper coffin.) Wesley wrote adoring letters to Mrs Pendarves, calling her 'Aspasia' and she replied in kind — or sufficiently so to ask later that he should burn her letters. Which he did – but only after copying them scrupulously.

He preached according to his appointment

Wesley was, however, a man of great faith, energy and persistence. On one of his 32 journeys into Cornwall he had made an appointment to preach at St Ives, and was behind schedule. In Redruth he had hired a local carriage and driver as he did not himself know the road; the driver's account of the journey has survived. In those days the main road forded the Hayle estuary at low tide, and they arrived too late for a safe passage. The driver was reluctant, and a local sailor warned them against trying, but Wesley put his head out of the carriage window and insisted, 'Take the sea, take the sea!'

'In a moment I dashed into the waves, and was quickly involved in a world of waters. The horses were now swimming, and the carriage became nearly overwhelmed by the tide, as its hinder wheels not infrequently merged into the deep pits and hollows in the sands. I struggled hard to retain my seat in the saddle, while the poor affrighted creatures were snorting in the most terrific manner, and furiously plunging through the opposing waves. I expected every moment to be swept into eternity, and the only hope I then cherished was on account of my driving so holy a man. At this awful crisis I heard Mr Wesley's voice. With difficulty I turned my head towards the carriage, and saw his long white locks dripping the salt sea down the rugged furrows of his venerable countenance. He was looking calmly forth from the windows, undisturbed by the tumultuous war of the surrounding waters, or by the danger of his perilous situation. He hailed me by a tolerably loud voice, and asked, "What is thy name, driver?" I answered, "Peter." "Peter," said Mr Wesley, "Peter, fear not, thou shalt not sink."

'With vigorous spurring and whipping I again urged on the flagging horses, and at last got safely over. We continued our journey and reached St Ives without further hindrance. We were both very wet, of course. Mr Wesley's first care, after his arrival, was to see me comfortably lodged at the tavern: he procured me warm clothes, a good fire and excellent refreshments. Neither were the horses forgotten by him. Totally unmindful of himself, he proceeded, wet as he was, to the chapel, and preached according to his appointment.'

Lemon squashed

'The Great Mr Lemon', who rose from bal-boy to be the richest man in Cornwall in the early eighteenth century, was not universally popular. On his death, Tristrem, the Truro sexton who (in the days before St Mary's even had a steeple) used to go from street to street with a bell to summon people to service, was ready to leap for joy when the great man died. Stamping on the vault where he'd laid Lemon low, he cried out in exultation, 'We've got him under now!'

Floored for words

A Methodist society was formed in Redruth in 1820, but the parson there who was also a magistrate (and therefore extremely powerful locally) determined to get rid of the sect. He appointed a day for the offenders to be brought before him, on charges which would have sent them to gaol. The courtroom was simply a room above the kitchen of the former 'Plume of Feathers' pub, beside the church. There was a large audience, since both well-wishers and ill-wishers wanted to see the proceedings. The clerk of the court and the reverend magistrate had just taken their chairs, when the floor suddenly gave way and descended into the kitchen in a cloud of dust and cries of panic. One gentleman cried out, 'Joe, where are we going?' But it proved to be a short journey, and amazingly no one was killed and no bones were broken.

The magistrate had lost his hat and wig, and the contents of his inkwell covered his face. As people gradually recovered from the shock, the Methodists who had been charged gathered round the magistrate to enquire what was to happen to them next. 'Go home,' he replied, 'go home. Sufficient unto the day is the evil thereof.'

One for the road

A certain gentleman not far from Penzance loved good liquor, and one evening had gathered some of his jovial companions together, determined to make a night of it. His wife, having had some experience of such gatherings, arranged for as much wine to be taken out of the cellar as she thought would be good for her husband and his companions. Safely locking the strong oak door of the cellar, she put the key in her pocket and went off to spend the evening with friends.

As the hours passed, she was inwardly congratulating herself on the success of her forethought when a heavy stumbling noise was heard on the stairs. Then two burly footmen staggered into her friends' living room, groaning under the weight of a ponderous cellar door, together with its door-frame, which had been sent by their master for the mistress kindly to unlock.